John Bufton

The Light of Eden and other Poems

John Bufton

The Light of Eden and other Poems

ISBN/EAN: 9783337253431

Printed in Europe, USA, Canada, Australia, Japan

Cover: Foto ©Thomas Meinert / pixelio.de

More available books at **www.hansebooks.com**

The Light of Eden

AND

OTHER POEMS.

BY

JOHN BUFTON.

"With silence only as their benediction
Thine angels come,
Where, in the shadow of some great affliction,
The soul sits dumb."

PRICE   -   HALF-A-CROWN.

Melbourne.

1890.

TO THE

REV. DR. PATON, M.A.,

PRINCIPAL OF NOTTINGHAM COLLEGE,

THESE POEMS ARE

𝔄𝔣𝔣𝔢𝔠𝔱𝔦𝔬𝔫𝔞𝔱𝔢𝔩𝔶 𝔍𝔫𝔰𝔠𝔯𝔦𝔟𝔢𝔡

BY

AN OLD STUDENT.

CONTENTS.

—:o:—

	PAGE.
THE LIGHT OF EDEN: OR, THE FIRST SACRIFICE	7
PRIZE ELEGY: TO A WELSHMAN ..	75
SOMETHING FAR AWAY	78
IN MEMORIAM: TO MY SUNDAY SCHOOL TEACHER	80
THE UNIVERSAL CREED ..	98
IN MEMORIAM: REV. J F. EWING, M.A.	100
WILD FLOWERS	102
WINTER: A SONG	104
SATURDAY EVENING: A SONNET	105
SWEET FLOWERS OF SPRING ..	106
THE SWALLOW	108
THE ROSE IN THE WOOD ..	109
SPRING ..	112
THE SHEPHERD OF RADNOR FOREST	115
CAMBRIA: A SONG ..	118
A SHOOTING STAR: A SONNET	120
THE AUSTRALIAN BLACK ..	121
AN AUSTRALIAN NATIONAL SONG	125
WAITING THE EVENTIDE	126
EARLY MORNING PRAYER. PSALM V. 3	128
ODE TO A BIRTHDAY	131
TO EVE'S FAIREST DAUGHTER ..	132
THE ORB OF NIGHT ..	134

THE LIGHT OF EDEN:

OR

The First Sacrifice.

I sing of human Hope the heaven of every man,
Of Doubt and Strife and Sin when human life began.
How beauteous was the dawn of those unclouded days
When man a King on earth knew but the speech of praise!
Alas, the morn is past, the noontide heat has come:
The God-like man rebelled: the "gods" are doomed to
    roam!
His lot unceasing toil, his home the desert wild;
Behold him wander forth, his partner and his child.

Another child is given; the weary years roll on;
The ancient Mother's hope clings round the younger son.
Pass on, ye hapless pair: the weary world is wide:
May Patience smooth your path, and Mercy be your guide.

The toils of day are done; the shades of evening close,
And Cain and Abel meet for converse and repose.
Each left his daily round, the flock was homeward driven,
When lo, an Angel came to speak the will of Heaven!
The pure and perfect man forsook the perfect Law,
And on his Maker's brow the frown of Justice saw;
But this could not abide, the sun must shine again,
For in the dawn of Time a Spotless Lamb was slain.
Now o'er the ancient hills a ray of hope appears,
And earth in speechless awe a precious promise hears.
The heavens in tempest veiled, a crown without a gem,
Reveal behind the storm the Star of Bethlehem.
Earth wipes away her tears, light streams across the world,
As to its eager gaze Heaven's Charter is unfurled.
The Arch has been designed, the Corner Stone is laid

To bridge the boundless chasm by disobedience made.
Before the hills were formed the plan of Grace was known,
Before seraphic forms bowed down before the throne.
The Wonder of the world, the Mystery sublime
Though planned in ancient days is for man's later time.

'Twas near the dreadful walls where earth received the
    curse.
The Angel came to man Heaven's message to rehearse.
The cherub at the gate with flaming sword was armed,
The next in robes of Peace. He cries: "Be not alarmed.
Attend the words of life, for life to man is given.
(Let earth in wonder stand, for silence reigns in heaven!)
The gift without a name on man has been bestowed,
The Prince of Life and Peace has taken up your load:
A Sacrifice for sin the Grace of God hath found,
And struck the note of peace which ever shall resound.
To Love's sublime appeal stern Justice lent an ear,
From Mercy's kindly eye stole down a crystal tear.
Then robed in leagues of light more glorious than the sun

The Prince of heaven drew near and cried, 'The work is
   done;
Behold I come, I come O God to do Thy will.'
While all the sons of God with bated breath stood still.
A Sacrifice was found, a Substitute complete,
And angels took their crowns and cast them at His feet.
The flaming sword was sheathed and placed in Mercy's
   hand,
And Love the sceptre swayed o'er all the ransomed land.
Thus Mercy conquest-crowned and Justice satisfied
Joined hands for evermore as bridegroom joined with bride.
To Him, the Prince of Peace, all tribes and tongues were
   given,
And louder than before burst forth the song of heaven.
Thus fades the primal law, the covenant is void,
For God shall yet be known and Satan's works destroyed.
The central heart of Love for man its blood will shed
And take away the curse that rests upon your head;
Arise thou son of man, let each an altar make
And from the gentle flock, for God, your victim take;

By blood is man redeemed, blood is the sacred price,
So shall ye offer up for sin your sacrifice."

So spake in solemn voice the messenger of light.
Then, as the lightning's flash, was hidden from their sight.
With hearts that throbbed aloud and eager, dazzled eyes
They gaze in silent awe away into the skies.
The shining form has gone, the voice is silent too,
Yet as a double star deep in the distant blue
The radiance floats afar where'er their eyes are turned,
Even on the rising moon the vision is discerned,
So dazzling were the wings that clave the evening air
That for a moment's space they saw them everywhere!

Calm was the listening night; no solitary sound
Fell on the ravished ear: dread silence reigned around,
Like some wierd realm where Death as monarch held the sway.
The orb of night arose, for he that lights the day
Had passed the western gate and fled away to rise

Beyond the shades of night to gladden other skies.

At length the younger spoke with low and reverent voice:
He said, "O brother Cain 'tis meet we should rejoice;
The Angel's holy words still lingering in mine ear
Contained no threat, no curse to fill the heart with fear:
The news that filled yon heaven with louder songs of praise
Should teach us sons of earth some feeble song to raise:
Lift up thy drooping head, compose thy troubled breast,
And speak our thanks to Heaven before we seek our rest.
Beside this sacred mount 'tis meet that we remain
And build our altars near when daylight comes again.
Bid brooding care be gone! Lo up yon azure steep
The lamp of night ascends and stars their vigils keep."

Cain sighs and lifts his head, and scans the boundless sky:
But higher than his sight his spirit's glances fly.
Beyond the spangled vault his vision soars afar,
And leagues beneath his feet appears the highest star.

He speaks in accents grave and tightly clasps his hands:
"Would that the solemn voice had issued forth commands
To follow him through space beyond yon lamps of heaven,
Or sit upon the clouds instead of what were given.
I care not for this wild ; life here is but a curse ;
And were there myriads more than this, none could be
    worse :
No happiness is mine in darkness or in light ;
The day is lone and long, and cheerless is the night.
The soil I daily till doth with reluctance give
Its lean and shrivelled fruit : 'twere better die than live !
Undone and cursed am I, a wanderer in the earth
Excluded from my home, the place that saw my birth.
I chafe and hunger here, my lot is hard to bear ;
O, for an angel's wing to quit this scene of care !
I'd quit the cursed orb and soar upon the wind,
And in my flight would leave the lightning's flash behind."

"Ah, brother dare not thus insult the Lord Most High,
While yet His chariot wheels are gleaming in the sky :

Lest He return again to justify His ways!
The earth His footstool is and showeth forth His praise.
And who art thou, O Cain, that thou shouldst thus complain
Against the Mighty One who over all doth reign?
Think on thy ways; repent: canst thou resist His might?
Be silent; seek thy rest until the morning light."

They lay them down to rest and kindly o'er them steals
Earth's benediction—sleep; and Night's still chariot wheels
Bring balm to weary hearts and bless the unborn day:
The distant stars grow dim and angels heard them say:
"We would not stay to see the evil deeds of men,
We hide behind the sun away from mortal ken."
Night's mantle slowly parts, the eastern sky grows pale,
Faint rays peep o'er the hills to wake the sleeping vale.
The morning breeze awakes and stirs the myriad leaves
Beneath whose guardian care Cain's sleeping bosom heaves.
The dewy veil of morn spreads through the twilight dim
And songsters in the grove commence their matin hymn.
The sunbeams scale the ridge that joins the eastern sky

And gild the topmost twigs unseen by human eye.

Cain opes his fiery eye and, gazing round awhile,

It lights on Abel's face and lo, it wears a smile.

He dreams, I wot, of flocks beside the limpid brook

While he is keeping watch in umbrageous nook,

A rich and goodly land clad in perennial green

Where tempests never come, earth's best and fairest scene.

Poor unambitious wight, resigned to any fate,

I envy not thy joys : be mine a higher state.

"Awake for day has come : arise, the morn is fair !

The lark is on the wing, his music fills the air."

He wakes with visage changed and says : " I would have slept

A sleep like this for aye : I dreamt that I had swept

Throughout the fields of space where night is never known :

No altar there appeared : none save a great white Throne.

A voice I heard afar as when deep thunder roars :

'Lift up your heads ye gates, ye everlasting doors

Give way and let the King, the King of Glory in.'

Then silence reigned awhile like that which follows sin :
'Ah, who is this that comes from Edom's plain' they cried,
'From Bozrah's battlefield with garments deeply dyed?'
'The King of Cherubim, the King in battle strong.'
The golden gates gave way and slowly passed along
The Conqueror and His Host, whilst angels lowly bowed.
He sate upon the throne amid the shining crowd,
When lo, a mighty voice : 'The victory is won,
All hail the Prince of Life, the Everlasting Son.'
I trembled as I gazed upon the stainless place,
While with his shining wings each angel veiled his face.
Yet all were happy there ; joy beamed in every eye ;
I woke and lo, the earth ! How near, to thought, the sky !"

Second Book.

Then Cain with anger moved: "thy visions—strange array—
Reflect the simple dreams that haunt thy mind by day.
They ill become thy years, but answer well thy birth,
Submissive son of toil, born to a blighted earth.
I knew and oft have spoke of scenes unknown to thee:
That home I yet will claim and test the dread decree.
Let worthier aims obtain and to my words attend:
Thy mother disobeyed, my father I defend.
The fault was truly small, if fault indeed there were:
If ought was ill for man why plant the poison there?
The rule of beast and bird was placed within our hands,
The flocks upon these hills, the life of other lands.
To rule the fertile earth and reign upon the sea
Implied, methinks, the right to every herb and tree.

Amid the myriad trees the fruit of one denied !
By such a lawless law must all the race abide ?
With universal choice is one restriction given ?
Unworthy then of Earth and more unworthy Heaven !

The heaven-born man partook with thanks his evening meal
Nor dreamt the downy fruit such poison could conceal
The helpmeet Heaven had given had culled at eventide
The best such light allowed as moon and stars supplied ;
She plucked in haste the fruit, 'twas Haste that wrought the
    ill—
The act of one right hand, no deed of conscious will.
For this our lordly sire is doomed henceforth to roam :
The earth he owned and ruled denies him now a home.
If Heaven has right to rule, the mighty to command
(And that alone is right that man can understand).
Its laws must plainly speak their origin divine ;
If harsh and meaningless they never shall be mine.
No power made Evil good since life and thought began,
And that is only Good that worketh good to man.

I knew not Right and Wrong : to me no charge was given,
Yet on my infant head fell fierce the curse of Heaven.
Can this be highest Good that worketh ill to me ?
O dire destroying Fate, I cannot bow to Thee ! "

  He paused nor sought reply : a tempest raged within :
The way of life is high, alas how near is sin !
The younger grieved and dumb with sadness on his brow
Attends his bleating flock until the sun is low.
Cain with his thoughts alone laments his hasty words,
But such a retrospect no guiding light affords.
Anon his doubts return, new questionings arise:
" The law was but a threat ; but is my anger wise ?"
The pensive shepherd comes, the sun is in the west,
And every little bird flies to its place of rest :
'Tis meet the elder son perform the sacred rite,
And raise the voice of praise to Him who made the light.
No prayer is in his heart, no praise upon his tongue ;
The younger bows alone, his soul with sadness wrung.

  Cain lays him down to sleep and darkness hides his frown ;

The breeze forgets to breathe, the silent stars look down.
On ancient Nature's breast, more kind than Doubt and Rage,
They lay their bodies down and dreams their thought engage.
Ah, blessed hours of rest to weary mortals given.
How welcome to the world, best gift and type of heaven!
Not only soothing man, but blessing flock and herd;
Outstretching as the heavens alike o'er beast and bird.
The sleeping earth is still and calm the arching sky
And God is over all a piercing sleepless Eye.
But ever night and day two angels watch and wait:
The messenger of Love, the harbinger of Hate.
Our daily thoughts decide which shall our steps attend;
We choose a deadly foe or find a faithful friend.
And chiefly while we sleep the spirit's door stands wide
And secret seeds are sown of envy, wrath, and pride.
Thus was it ere the dawn had flushed the orient sky;
The Tempter found a throne with none to occupy.
With unabated skill his deadly craft is plied,
While in the Doubter's heart the fuel is supplied.
Receptive is the soil, prepared for Envy's seeds:

Designed for fruits of Praise, behold it crowned with weeds!

Cain dreamt a horrid dream framed by the Foe of Man,
And surging through his soul these wild suggestions ran:
"Thou wast not born to serve, thou art a prince on earth;
Seek pleasure, take thine ease, exhaust the fount of myrth.
Let Heaven attend its own, the spacious earth is thine.
Regard no tyrant's threat, be free and thus divine!
No power can change the will: make it thy law and lord
Let Heaven hurl darts of fire, the thunder be His word:
He triumphs evermore who to himself is true,
And Hope guilds every lot with fair unfading hue.
Heaven drove thee from thy home an unoffending child
And with its scorching curse made earth a wasted wild.
Thy father led thee forth in fancied guilt and shame;
But what is change of place if thou art still the same?
The portal may be barred: the mind defies the sword
And still those scenes are thine in Memory safely stored.
Go forth in conscious strength thy own high thought thy
    stay

Spurn from thee empty dread, hold on thy chosen way!"

Such was the fiery train that lit his gloomy soul.
And many a black resolve across his visage stole.
O restless son of Time night brings for thee no peace
While e'en the fowl of heaven their wanderings nightly
  cease!
But thou with face divine and thoughts that haunt the spheres
Dost find no resting place 'midst strife and want and tears.
The earth beneath thy head enjoys serene repose
And o'er the silent scene still Night her mantle throws.
In all the living earth, throughout the stellar plains,
O'er all save man alone a nightly Sabbath reigns.
The downy hand of Sleep has sealed old Nature's eye
But thou, O Heaven-born soul, must dream and start and
  sigh!
The stars begin to fade, the breeze of morning blows
And in the eastern sky the crown of morning glows,
And fairer grows the dawn and vocal wood and dell
Whilst joyful Nature sings: "He hath done all things well."

How tranquil was the night, how gladsome is the morn!
But ah! the night has gone; another day is born.
Alas that light should hide the jewelled crown of night:
Is it Thy glory, Lord, that hides Thee from our sight?

Behold the sleepers lie unconscious side by side
The children of one sire, one mother's hope and pride:
Bound by the bond of blood, in each a human heart:
By Nature's ties how near: in soul how far apart!
Type of the troubled world: one heaven above us all;
To savage and to sage one world-embracing call.
Sleep on and take your rest! Blow soft ye winds of heaven,
For this is God's great day, most sacred of the seven:
A picture kept for man of peaceful Eden gone,
A promise that again lost Eden shall be won.
Sleep on unless His praise already moves your breast,
Unless there dawns within a holy Sabbath rest.
Keep silence sinful man till praise attune thy tongue:
God's praises shall not fail, His glory be unsung!

The rising light of morn unlocks the younger's eye:

"Hail peaceful dawn," he said, "hail herald of the sky!
O Light behind all Light, illumine and inspire
That I may see Thy Truth and it alone desire!
Methinks that Thou dost hear though hidden from my sight;
For what to me is dark, to Thee, perchance. is Light
I know not where Thou art, Thy path I cannot trace,
But did not man—my sire—speak with Thee face to face?
The hunger of my heart is surely known to Thee,
Still would I see Thy face; but who Thy face can see?
The angel's dread behest I hasten to obey
Thine altar I will build, my bleating victim slay."

He seeks his eager flock that sweep the dewy ground;
From duty more than choice he makes his Sabbath round.
God ceased His former works but worketh hitherto,
His ancient Energies flow forth in channels new:
Since man stood forth complete the Sabbath reigned above;
Of old He wrought through Law, but now He works by
    Love.
His Sabbath is not sleep, His work is ever blest;

Redemption is not toil ; to ransom is to rest.
So goes the shepherd forth until the lost is found,
To liberate the lamb in tangled thickets bound ;
'Tis Mercy moves His feet : Compassion leads the way ;
Who blesses in the morn is blessed throughout the day.

Meanwhile the elder wakes ; no music fills the air ;
The Sabbath ! Not for him, nor praise, nor even prayer.
The visions of the night his waking thoughts approve
And up the heights of Hate the horrid legions move.
The weary hours pass on and pride and passion burn.
He bids his doubts begone : with clamour all return.
" Is this the day of rest ? another ancient curse !
The mind left to its thoughts but makes the tedium worse.
But lo, the stream flows on ; each beast pursues his way :
I see without no change ; 'tis but a common day.
Ah me ! a mocking lie : my only rest is toil
My curse must be my crown ; my joy to till the soil !"
And thus the Day of days wore on to eve unblest ;
Unhallowed in his heart it brought no balm of rest.

In earnest thought and praise the younger spent the day,
Thought o'er their sacrifice and mourned the long delay.
The mandate both received, but neither understood
The mystic tale of Love, its inner soul of Good.
For them the plain command; the promise for the race:
And willing hearts and pure shall ever see His face.
The promise dimly lived, for duty filled their mind:
The promise rests with God the duty with mankind.
How little yet we know when types have passed away
Of how the countless worlds may bless that early day!
The Wonder of that day is still the Mystery,
The Star of Hope that shines o'er Time's dark surging sea.

Third Book.

Who that is pure in heart but knows the mystic power
That binds us to the brook and weds us to the flower?
Communing in our heart with Nature's secret soul
We feel the thrilling pulse that throbs throughout the whole.
The very silence speaks the sacred Truth of things
And thus we soar to Heaven on Nature's helpful wings.
But man comes nearer God in contact with his kind,
And thought the swifter flows when mind engages mind.
Hence each the other seeks at early eventide.
There's joy in human speech unknown until denied:
The prisoner in his cell of every voice bereft
Would choose the very lash to have this freedom left.

Each has his burning thought a burden or a joy,
For through the sacred hours high themes their mind
    employ.
The younger thus began : "How blest the power of thought
Whereby each passing hour with new delight is fraught !
It gives the valleys voice and makes the darkness light ;
The flowers are smiles of day, the dew-drops tears of night.
The beast sees but the ground : he never lifts his eye
Above the grassy plain, nor heeds the distant sky.
Desire for food and rest, the circle of his sense

He lives, a soulless thing—no hope and no suspense.
But speech, the gift of Heaven, the garment of our thought,
Proclaims our high descent—a lesson daily taught.
All pleasures of the mind the gracious purpose prove
Of Him whose breath we are, in Whom we live and move.
But chiefly does this day declare Him Wise and Good,
And bear a thousand hopes yet dimly understood."

To which, with speaking eye the elder thus replies :
"Thy mild, submissive words are more devout than wise.

To think is but to face a thousand ills in store,
And bear again to-day the ills endured before.
Ah, Thought! 'tis great indeed, at once our crown and curse,
Of Hate, and Hope, and Pride, old Nature's faithful nurse.
The power perchance were good, if ought indeed there were
In Memory or in Hope to banish brooding care.
But what to memory dear sleeps in the tragic past?
Its whispered glories fade, its thunders only last.
The magic wand of words reveals man's noble birth,
Reveals a God-like gift, and marks him lord of earth.
And thus it was at first, Dominion's triple crown:
To name, command, converse and hand the story down.
But Time revealeth much: a wider knowledge came,
And now it serves to tell the story of his shame:
The shame he never earned; but heaped upon his head;
Of Wisdom and of Good 'twere better nothing said!
Is laughter lofty speech? 'tis but a sunlit peak
Clad in eternal snow; how beautiful, how bleak!
Above, the sunny smile; below, the chilling tear:
The merry laughter there; the bitter weeping here!

No creature laughs for joy? Perchance: nor does he weep;
Man's joy is seldom high; his sorrow oft is deep.
'Tis not the instrument, but what it does for man
That shows its true intent and marks the primal plan.
Thou speakest of this day as more than others blest:
What blessing does it bring? no day can give man rest.
His rest, if rest there be, is in himself alone,
In toil, and thought, and quest to find the yet unknown.
The princely powers of man but mock his present state,
And serve with fiercest scorn to curse his cruel fate;
Unblest, except wherein they give him power to rise
On self-supporting thought, and circumstance despise."

And speaking thus he ceased. The hush of twilight reigned
Ill suiting angry words: in silence both remained.
How solemn is the hour that marks the close of day
For Time, what man calls time, flies on its trackless way!
In silence darkness comes with rest upon its wings,
And hides the works of man to show us better things.

His works shine in the earth, His wisdom in the sky ;
But man perceives them not till Heaven adjusts his eye.
And as the sacred veil in Israel's holy tent
Shut out the vulgar gaze, so is the darkness meant.
The day, the outer court ; the eve, the middle wall ;
The night the inner space, the Holiest of all :
Beyond the twilight shade, within this sacred place
The Priesthood of pure hearts may pass and see His face.
Who has the open eye may nightly yet behold
That Vision wonderful, Shechinah as of old.
It lights the dome of Heaven, the Temple of mankind
With Wisdom for the heart and Wonder for the mind.

The darkness denser grew, the silence more profound :
'Twas not a time for words, but speech without the sound
When suddenly the breeze spread out the shepherd's locks
Like some wild waving tuft the crown of craggy rocks,
And snapped the airy train of solemn rever'e :
In reverent tones he spoke of man and Deity :
" The majesty of man reveals itself herein ;

The second self of God, he still has power to sin !
Endowed with perfect powers he leaves the certain way
And, seeking secret paths, goes consciously astray.
The very power of choice the choosing even ill
Before the perfect good, declares a God-like will.
The evil use and curse show not the Giver's plan,
The power marks Heaven's design, the use belongs to man.
Our restlessness and want flow from an evil choice
And then we slander Heaven with haughty impious voice.
The greatest gifts misused the greatest evils bring
While simple Faith and Hope find good in everything ;
'Tis folly to complain : our lot is not unblest,
For day finds happy toil and night brings welcome rest.
Methinks the angel spoke of 'blessings yet in store :'
We know not what of good may wait us on before ;
This lesson let me learn : how little yet I know,
And trust the Torch of Time the hidden things to show."

He ceased, for Cain asleep began to dream aloud
And quiet lightning leaped along a chain of cloud,

While oft a spreading flash gleamed up the leaning sky
The restless dreamer sighed and closed the inner eye:
Some fragment of his thoughts expressed in waking hours
Broke like the lightning's flash forth from his sleepy powers.
The shepherd's sleepless eye attends the darting light;
In lonely speechless awe he contemplates the sight:
"How glorious are His works alike by night and day,
Minute beside our feet, majestic far away!
Yon starry line outstretched across the dome of night
Must be, methinks, His path amid the worlds of light,
Or where the angel host march on their silent round
To bear the will of Heaven to Nature's utmost bound.
Perchance assemble there upon the spacious plain
The great embattled host that guard the high domain.
The countless flock of stars that stray above my head
Oppress my struggling thought with awe and holy dread.
Great must that Shepherd be who calleth each by name,
And guides their silent course, from Whom at first they came!
Yon pale ascending moon though nearer seems more strange:
At first a crescent streak it shines its round of change.

Mayhap the changing earth controls whate'er is near
The moon, the moving cloud, the seasons of the year,
The leafy woods of Spring and Summer's golden fields
While even human thought to change and doubting yields.
But yonder distant lights for signs and seasons given
Unchanged delight the earth and deck the floor of heaven.
I watch their wheeling flight the vast harmonious train
And think, O Miracle, His ancient thought again!"

With such reflections filled he lays him down to sleep
And prays the God of heaven his life to guide and keep,
Thus ends the Sabbath day in pious thought and prayer
And God's good angel comes to keep him in His care.

Shall He no entrance gain who made the human mind
Whilst man, untutored man, holds converse with his kind?
Shall He who built the soul find no access thereto?
He hath His secret door, His sacred avenue.
Yea, divers spirits come and gaze and give and go;
They haunt the heart of man in ways he does not know.

To those who fear His name He makes His secret known,
And never leaves the pure to seek and grope alone
So with that blameless soul the Keeper of the sheep
In that pathetic dawn : He bade His angel sweep
The gathering clouds away and liberate the light.
And truths unheard before were told to man that night :
" The Source and Soul of all, the Primal Fount of Power
Revealed His Robe of light : 'twas Nature's natal hour.
His thought the law of things, the present Order grew ;
The inner Force unchanged evolved in aspects new.
Within the Chaos wild one changeless purpose beat
The steady Pulse of Life that Chance shall ne'er defeat.
The lonely Æons passed, a higher order came,
And tides of Being flowed and passed without a name.
The Ancient Thought of God grew clearer age by age
And fairer forms arose at each advancing stage.
At length the living frame erect and godlike stood :
Heaven breathed the breath of life, and all was—' very
    good '

These were Creation's days, God's great millennial days
Unmeasured by the sun, ungladdened by his rays.
Henceforth His Sabbath reigns throughout the age of Man,
For God finds rest and joy in Love's redemptive plan.
Thus came the world from God, the vesture of His thought
And man the highest last to crown the whole was brought.
The earth was made for man, the world and man for God
And Heaven for sons of Light, His messenger's abode.
For in the dawn of Time the Mighty Elohim
Begirt the Throne around with saints and Seraphim
His highest care is man, the Ruler on the earth,
Designed for higher things accordant with his birth :
On him the angels wait, o'er him were tears in heaven
For him shall Mercy plead that sin may be forgiven,
That Love may overcome and human discord cease
And ill be crowned with good in everlasting peace."

Such were the glimpses given in visions of the night
Of things beyond the range of timebound mortal's sight.

There lives within the mind a quenchless thirst to know
The source whence all things come and whither all things go.

We rise from out the Past, dim distant motherland:
The shadowy Future comes, and who shall take our hand
Amid the gathering clouds and lead us into light?
Our life is as a day—at either end the night.
Each day a rising rock above the sea of seas
That marks the ebb and flow of two Eternities.
Is man the great Perhaps, the foam upon the shore
Borne from the sea of Chance to perish evermore?
His body owns the earth, but whence the dreaming soul?
The grave demands his dust: is this the spirit's goal?
He reads the riven rocks, he questions heaven and earth:
They tell no certain tale of purpose, age, or birth,
While of his destiny they have no tale to tell
For Nature knows no heaven and man created hell.
Where then is knowledge found and where the place of light
Since it is hid from man, from every creature's sight?
As comes the light from far the common light of day
So comes the light divine from Truth's eternal Ray.
A clearer day has dawned and shines upon us now,

And yet the creed of man is only " Who ?" and " How ?
He climbed from " What ?" and " Where ?" to this sublimer
  height
And still the prophets die with prayer *Mehr Licht*, "more
  Light!"

Cain had his dream of Truth, a vision of the whole ;
His Guardian kept the gate, the entrance of his soul.
He wove his gaudy web : behold the Cosmos rise !
Old Chaos feels his touch and owns him lord of lies.
'Tis meet that man should know the things that went before ;
Who knows not whence he is is cheated evermore.
Know then that Nature was before aught else began,
' Eternal, not of time,' the feeble phrase of man !
For had there nothing been then could there nothing be,
Nor light, nor seeing eye, nor aught for eye to see ;
But hoary Nature *is* and hence it ever WAS,
It knew no origin, no 'antecedent cause.'
Its own inherent force, the Primal Energy
Evolved this ordered world and all the worlds we see

A thousand forms it wore while stormful Æons passed
And each in order rose more perfect than the last
Then moving life appeared a quivering conscious 'cell'
Whence flowed the stream of life as water from a well :
In many streams it flowed, with varying speed they ran :
From this high spirits came; from that the brute and man,
But from a starry dust, the ancient Nebulæ
Arose whate'er has been and whatso'er shall be.
And Him ye name Supreme is but the Flower of all
Whom ages yet unborn *To Pan*, the Whole, will call.
And being thus the Sum of Nature and the soul
Man is a part of Him who only is the whole ;
And no inferior part subservient to the Head
Unfit to breathe His name save with a guilty dread
One nature makes us one in Source and Soul akin
Hence none has right to rule and none can ever sin :
Not one in numbered years, not one in cruel might,
Yet Time is but a name and rule is never right.

In knowledge ye are young unlike the Powers on high
But time will make you one : *eritis sicut Di*.
All worship lies herein : in wonder at the Great :
Its life is Ignorance—your present pious state.
And that is ever great whatever is unknown :
A thing to bow before with meek beseeching moan !
But growing knowledge kills the creed of yesterday
And frames a freer Faith from Reason's crystal Ray.
These spectres of the mind shall vanish with the light
And Superstition sink in blank Oblivion's night.

And wherefore bow to Him ye meekly call Most High?
His cruel power I own, His goodness I deny :
The pure eternal Good no Being yet attained
'Tis but an empty thought unproved and unexplained.
Thy blinded brother bows before the ancient Power
And drones his pious song through every waking hour :
Thy argument may fail and Reason vainly plead

But Ridicule shall test the fibre of his creed.
He builds his broad-based faith on ' Beauty and Design.'
In Nature's perfect frame—for him a thing divine !

But these are in the eye and rise within the brain :
He sees the thing he thinks and thinks and sees again.
But Nature made itself with here and there a flaw :
Remorseless in its rule, resistless in its law.

'Tis not a father's work of tenderness and tears,
But stern and strong throughout, unheeding hopes or fears.

The ordered seasons come and keep their ancient course ;
The Summer breeze is soft, the Winter winds are hoarse.

Behold the hungry beast that prowls the gloomy wood :
He slays the straying lamb for lack of other food :

Each has his deadly foe through all the chain of life ;
The highest lives in fear, the lowest shares the strife.

The fittest thus survive : the march is ever on
With shriek, and groan, and gasp till every flaw be gone :

But ye are asked to slay, with prayer and solemn rite,
The choicest of the flock, and burn it in His sight !

Ye speak of aim and end, the 'law of final cause,'
And seek one fixed 'result' from complicated laws !

Ye find the end ye seek, but other ends are there :
The claws that feed the beast his bleeding brother tear.

The sense that gives delight, gives anger, shame and pain ;
'Tis folly thus to boast, and idle to complain.
The Power that works the Good, works equally the ill.
It bids you feed the flock, then, brute-like, catch and kill !
'Tis kind and tender here, a thirsty Tyrant there :
To-day it fills with Hope, to-morrow blank Despair.
The changing good and ill are Nature's smile and frown ;
But man has power to rise and tread oppression down.
Then be thy only God thy own almighty will
That laughs at chance and change, and welcomes good or ill !"

 Thus ends the dream of things, the vision of the past :
The true, perchance, will pass, the false will doubtless last.
The ways of God are high above our noblest thought,
And break our systems down, our theories bring to nought.
His path is hid from man who roams, a child, abroad ;
But happy if our thought in reverence rise to God.
The seas and hoary hills, the darkness and the light.
Are surely shadows of the Nameless Infinite.
This moving dream of sense is but the thought of God,
Eternal if He wills, blank nothing at His nod !

For man a floating song, a broken melody—
Itself the perfect chord, the soul of Harmony.
The mystery of pain appals the tender heart,
That magnifies a sigh, and dreads a passing smart.
Our sympathy is moved, and judges not with truth :
It looks on bending age, and not on buoyant youth.
But life is full of good when Wisdom is our guide,
And joy may light our path, though health may be denied.
The pangs and pains of earth are not the pains of one :
Each has his pain and joy, a gasp and all is done :
There is no sum of sense, no huge impersonal pain ;
The ills of yesterday are not endured again.
And man, far-seeing man with keener pangs and fears
Lives but from pulse to pulse, and not in crowded years.
The ills are soon forgot in life's full joyous tide :
The discords daily die, the harmonies abide.

The glorious dawn is here, its peace to Heaven akin.
The dewdrops hold the sky, the lightning lurks within.

Each grasps the flashing fire and binds the distant sun
Within its crystal heart—a world in every one!
The pulse of one great life beats in each rising blade,
And thrills the meekest flower that blushes in the glade.
Resistless forces fly swift-winged above, below:
Each keeps its ordered course where Wisdom bids it go:
Through stars and suns they sweep in spheres unseen, remote;
Each plays its perfect part without a jarring note.
Fresh is the rosy morn, and fair the rising day,
Pure as the purling brook that sings its winding way.

  Perplexed with crowding thoughts the brothers greet the light,
And nurse the knowledge gained in visions of the night.
These were the days of light when Wisdom blossomed forth,
And things concealed in heaven were shown to man on earth.
The mystery of the past was mastered in a day,
The stream of future thought began its endless way.
The childhood of the race is like to that of men:
It learns each opening year as much as other ten.

Filled with sublimer thoughts, they lived a larger life ;
But knowledge oft has brought, instead of concord, strife.
Each yearned to tell his tale, not knowing whence it came—
These were not days of books or battles for a name—
How full of zeal is thought! a restless urgent thing !
It dies in stagnant swamps, lives only on the wing.
The younger breathes his prayer bowed prostrate to the earth;
The elder, unabashed, displays unseemly mirth !
Their morning duties press ; each goes his quiet round :
One bound to seek his flock, and one to till the ground.
Unblest is he who leaves the common lot undone ;
And each may find his task : it calls to every one.
'Tis said the ground was cursed, and slowly yields her fruit :
For him 'tis doubly cursed who lives below the brute
That only feeds and sleeps, and neither works nor prays ;
Man ! See thy blushing hand : arise and mend thy ways !
The pressing duty done, they meet when noon is high ;
In earnest intercourse the crowded moments fly.
The elder, as was meet, began the high discourse :
He spake of Time and Change, and Law controlling Force.

The whole adjusted world where Thought and Order shine
Displayed for him no proof of forethought or design:
"And if there were a Power that made the world and man,
Who ordered Force and Life, since life on earth began,
He cannot be the Best, for pain and want abound
Through every hour the sun speeds on his constant round.
And if He were Supreme, there were no place for sin:
For He who ordered all, brought good and evil in.
But Thought, the flower of all, is Nature's perfect child:
Man thinks as Thought is given in native wisdom wild;
His good his only God; desire, his only law.
What Nature prompts is right, for Nature knows no flaw.
Man measures this and that, and seems to make a choice.
What other could he do? Compulsion gave him voice.
Whatever is is right, but each has some desire,
The brute, as well as man: the son, as well as sire.
Thou hast thy pious thought; thy thought is right to thee:
I know a deeper truth, and that is right to me.
And yet I think and choose: 'tis more than strange, I grant,
And hard to call that good which brings me work and want.

How can my will be free   I came from out the past ;
I cannot alter that : it evermore will last.
The thing that gives me pain is not a choice of mine ;
And after choosing well, I oftentimes repine.
Then Fear sometimes alarms, and Hope my bosom swells :
It cannot but be so : necessity compels."

In such poor words he spake of things beyond his ken,
Of things that to this day are hidden deep from men.
For who can trace the source of any passing thought ?
Man chose a year ago what now he sets at nought.
And is he not the same, the Ego of the past ?
And does he not remain the same unto the last ?
The same with other thoughts : he knows not whence they
        come :
The night is very dark : the child is far from home.

How great the mind of man. an everlasting " Why ?"
That questions Thought itself, an Eye within the eye!

It roams the Field of Space, and haunts the night of Time ;
Its work, a second world ; its very wreck, sublime !
But Truth has much to tell, and Heaven is very high,
And men, like gods of old, in vain attempt the sky.
To questions asked of yore hoarse echoes yet respond,
And Reason's highest flight but shows the heights beyond.
Let Science lift her torch and Knowledge fly abroad—
The world is still for man the Seamless Robe of God :
Let Wonder pass away: it comes to life again,
For Earth is ever new as to the first of men.

At length the younger spake : emotion burdened speech :
" 'Tis wrong methinks to grasp at things beyond our reach ;
The truth we need to know will doubtless be made known.
I'll use the light I have, and leave my doubts alone.
The mystery of my choice I cannot fathom now.
I choose and am content : I leave the hidden · How ?"
The thing of doubtful face, howe'er the judgment rise,
Is wholly wrong to me, though good in other eyes :

And if I heed it not but follow Passion's lead
My spirit burns within and smiles not on the deed.
There surely is for man a perfect Law and Guide
That clamours for the right and will not be denied.
The thing beyond my power, however black it be
In other eyes than mine is never wrong to me.
He who is over all will surely never ask
The thing impossible, the more than human task.
He only asks, I wot, alike of me and thee
The homage of the heart in conscious liberty.
I know not all His ways: He surely knows the best:
I'll give the offering asked and leave to Him the rest.
I cannot fathom Time, the nameless night of yore,
My thought demands a start and then 'what went before?'
I cannot measure Space or fix its gloomy bound:
The eye would see the end: the mind still looks beyond.
I cannot think of one and hide the other view—
The end, there is no end: they cannot both be true!
They are, methinks, a part of Him who is the All:
'Tis great and wonderful, and man is very small.

D

And yet there shines herein some nobleness of mind
That man discerns the night and is not wholly blind.

   Creation's ample song has one small plaintive strain
That rises from the earth of sorrow, want and pain ;
But shadows must attend the brightness of the sun,
The two are ever joined : we cannot have the one.
The passing pangs and pains alike of man and beast
But whet the appetite for Joy's abounding feast.
The aim and end of pain are hidden deep from man,
But judge it not in haste, 'tis Heaven's mysterious plan.
The earth supplies the want of every living thing :
The beast goes forth content, the bird on joyful wing,
Their life, the passing day, their present wants are few,
And ever with the day its bounty comes anew.
With life and daily food what more can creature need?
To breathe the breath of Life is happiness indeed.
But He who framed the earth hath strewn with lavish hand
Not only herb and tree o'er all the fruitful land,
But Beauty walks abroad in mead and leafy bower :
Far from the eye of man He plants the lonely flower.

Not food for common want, but beauty everywhere—
Ah, surely He is good who made the world so fair!
How sweet the fragrant bud that blushes into bloom
Alike on mountain side and in the thicket's gloom!
Behold it's perfect form! The beast will pass it by
Unfit for common food : not so the seeing eye.
Perchance the straying flock have eyes for beauty, too,
And note the humble flower that bends beneath the dew.
No heedless hand is here in each up-springing gem
That sits a matchless thing upon its modest stem.
No evil thought is here but only purest love ;
Heaven kisses earth herein : 'tis something from above!
The panting hart may haste impatient to the stream
But man with double joy : there's gladness in its gleam.
A mute eternal song floats on through brake and lea
That soothes the restless thought that grasps at Mystery.
On every side I mark the perfumed Hand of God
And think I trace the prints where Holy Feet have trod ;
There's order for the mind and beauty for the eye,
And wherefore is it thus if Good be but a lie?

Methinks He still walks forth in yon enchanting spot :
The Lord is surely here and we have known it not !
There's music in the air, the hum of happy life ;
How grand the psalm of joy ; how few the tones of strife !
There's beauty, peace and song : behold the perfect plan—
The glory of Himself, the happiness of man !"

So spake the pious heart of him who never knew
The happy Paradise that passed from mortal view.
He mourns not o'er the past, his hope is on before :
Lost Eden's gate is closed, he seeks another door.
Cain wondered at the words which left his brother's tongue:
" 'Twas like my mother's song when I was very young.
The Lord hath haply spoke this wisdom in his ear
And left me to my dreams that fill my soul with fear.
'Tis not his native thought, nor hath he eyes to see
In all the changeful world such hidden harmony.
Whence then this deeper truth, by whom such lessons
    taught ?

Have angels shown him this?   I cannot brook the
    thought!"
Such were the rapid thoughts that stirred his jealous heart:
He fain would find the truth yet bade the truth depart.
Ah man, thou walking want, thou Sum of all desire
And only great herein : a clod enclosing fire ;
Too great to know how great, unique upon the earth
Thy explanation, God, and Heaven thy place of birth!

  Again the younger speaks, and day is now far spent :
" Our solemn duty waits, my soul is ill content.
We pine for fuller light to light the path we go.
And yet from day to day neglect the thing we know :
We seek a clearer light, a greater good we crave,
And still despise and spurn the present good we have!
The only service asked with hopeful promise given
Remains, alas, undone despite offended Heaven.
The way of light methinks is near the humble road
Where meek obedience walks and seeks the hand of God.
Our sacred altar waits : this night must see it built
Or on our guilty head shall rest a greater guilt.

To both the same command, to both one promise given,
Hence should we side by side observe the will of Heaven."
To which the elder thus with milder look and voice :
" The task were quickly done if only done from choice.
Together have we lived and wandered far and wide,
'Twere ill perchance to part and in this act divide :
Thy pious wish prevails and not my own desire :
But why a living thing devoted to the fire ?
And least of all the lamb deserves such cruel fate
But wherefore snatch the life of creature small or great ?
Has Heaven not given them life, to which, like man, they
  cling ?
Who slays a speechless brute must do a horrid thing ! "
 Then Abel : " Woe is me if I should disobey :
Who gave the creature life may take that life away.
'Tis not the deed of man for Heaven directs his hand ;
Obedience now were best : we yet may understand.
Let us our altars raise upon the grassy mound ;
For day is dying fast, the dew is on the ground."

Cain finds a massive stone, which, with superior skill
To fabled Sisyphus, he forces up the hill
The tiller of the ground with Herculean might
Attains the sacred mount beneath the waning light.
With princely dignity the practised hand of toil
As with a giant's stroke removes the stubborn soil ;
The monolith is fixed like some uplifted rock
While Abel's gathered stones seem like his folded flock
As yet a scattered heap.   He lays them side by side
A double cubit long, two sacred cubits wide.
The skill his hand may lack the heart can well supply,
And what delights the heart will ever please the eye.
A double cubit high : his own right arm the rule,
For earth's first architect had framed no cunning tool.
Behold the structure rise four square upon the sod
First Temple in the earth, first altar unto God !

Fourth Book.

How happy is the heart in holy rites employed !
There springs the nameless peace that fills the inmost void.
The life is then complete : all past and future good
Is narrowed to an hour and Heaven is understood.
Small joy the elder feels in this his work begun,
Although he looks with pride on what his hands have done.
They leave the sacred hill and seek their wonted place ;
But darkness hides the joy that beams in Abel's face.
Lo, on the distant mount that props the southern sky.
A sight unseen before attracts the eager eye :
Their new-made altars rise above the dim dark land :
The azure wall behind and stars as sentries stand ;
Between, in rainbow form, a rising light appears !
And soon a waning moon their awe struck spirit cheers.

The ruddy orb grows pale in climbing up the night
And sheds upon the scene a calm benignant light.
While o'er one altar shines the bold bright star of even :
A promise, haply, this of sacred fire from heaven.
In silent wonder each beholds the omen rise
Majestic, calm and clear, the jewel of the skies.
How peaceful is the hour in solemn silence deep !
But sleep must overcome, the silent victor sleep.
One word the elder speaks in lying down to rest :
" The star arose on thee : Heaven deems thy work the best.'

Their guardian angels come and ever as before
The key of kindred thought unlocks the inmost door.
The Angel of the Lord encampeth ever near
The humble and the pure who sojourn in His fear,
He hallowed Abel's heart and fed the fount of dreams
That bathed his thirsting thought in fresh celestial streams.
" 'Tis well, thy thought is well unknowing to obey,
For duty lives in light, the daughter of the day.

And like the orb of heaven shines ever day and night
Though half its blazing path is hid from human sight.
And light shall ever guide the pilgrim on the road
Who, like the glowworm, toils nor spurns his light from God
The will of Gracious Heaven ye hasten to obey
This night ye cannot hear : it waits a future day.
But morning mists shall melt, the sun of Truth arise,
The brightness of whose day shall gladden many eyes.
But learn, O son of man, the whole round world is one ;
The fevered pulse of pain descends from sire to son.
The nameless host of life that breathe the vital air,
Expectant wait in hope with man, Creation's heir.
The whole Creation groans in Sin together bound ;
But Heaven will hear the sigh, and heal the hidden wound.
The lofty and the low, the beautiful and base.
All range around a Man, the Root of every race.
The First-born of the whole, the Author of the whole
Shall come to conquer sin, and ransom every soul.
No garland on His brow, a servant shall He come,
And, showing men the way, shall lead the Nations home.

He is the way of life ; redemption lies herein :
To seek each others good ; by love to conquer sin."

Hail day of human hope ! Hail Preparation Eve !
Earth's second birthday, thou, the light of all that live.
From thee the Star of Hope has never ceased to shine
O'er all the darkened world : oft dim, but still divine.

The Powers of Darkness hold the "Court of Human
    Blood,"
(The first in Eden sat : the third approved the Flood) :
A tempest raged therein, and tossed its waves of bile.
While from each flaming eye flashed forth a cunning smile.
Then rose Diabollos, who slandered Heaven of old ;
The senate howled applause, and bade their chief unfold
The purpose of his heart to hearts that know not fear.
They cease, for Satan's voice makes each an open Ear.
" Immortals ! Unsubdued ! Great deeds invite us all..
And who shall fail or fear who can no further fall ?
Swear as ye did of old by Hell's deep cavern gloom :
· To hate the Good and God, my duty and my doom !"

One battle made us free, though overcome by might,
The next by guile was gained and guile must win to-night.
Attend your Leader's flight where yonder altars rise
'Tis thither Duty calls, 'tis there that Glory lies!"
The solemn senate rose: deep groans approve the plan.
Then silently they sped to test the second man.
" The wish of Cain is well to offer sacrifice:
'Twas half the truth that cost the peace of Paradise "
So spake the ancient Prince, alighting on the ground,
And marshalling his host in many ranks around.
He fills the sleeper's mind with germs of loyalty:
" Obedience oft is best and now is best for thee:
Obey and be thou blest or find that none can bless,
And once for all fulfil the law of righteousness.
Give what thy hands have raised, the first fruits of the ground,
Nor wish what is not thine, a creature bruised and bound.
Heaven cannot ask of thee what is not thine to give
But what Himself has given, 'tis meet He should receive.
With solemn mein withal perform the sacred rite,
And thee and thine shall find acceptance in His sight.

'Tis fit that thou be first in honour as in age
And thus in years to come adorn the sacred page.
Thy brother's keeper, too : and thou the elder son,
'Tis thine to choose the time this duty shall be done.
Be worthy of thy birth, a son of Paradise,
The first in seeking truth, the first in sacrifice."

A tempest raged that night fierce in the upper air
That roused the sleeping brook and wrecked the lion's lair :
It broke the buding flower and bruised the golded fruit
Inflicting grief on man and gladness on the brute :
It bathed the thirsting earth and made the valleys sing
But spoiled the food of man and every tender thing.
Through clouds the morning dawned but all was pure and still
Except the roaring brook and every rushing rill.
Uprising each prepares the gift that Heaven demands.
Cain hastened to the field : the labour of his hands
He fain would offer up : but all the purest, best,
Is blemished, broken, spoiled ! "Go offer Heaven the rest,

'Tis still the best thou hast," a voice within him said,
" And thou art not to blame for Forces overhead :
The storm is with the Powers that rule in fields above ;
They send whiche'er they list : the vulture or the dove."
He plucks the dripping fruit and bears it to the hill.
And hastens to be first this duty to fulfil.
He lays them on the stone in tiers of gold and green.
With many a flower and herb in fragrant rows between.
No crackling thorns are sought, nor pitch nor scented pine
For all their fire is quenched by Heaven's untimely rain.
Fair is the mingled mass of foliage, fruit and flower :
Can Heaven reject such gifts, the gems of field and bower ?
But, Abel going forth bows down in secret prayer:
" Most High and Holy One may we Thy mercy share :
Regard us and the gifts we offer up to-day
And lead us evermore in Thine appointed way."
He binds a blameless lamb and leads it to the place
Where God, perchance, will speak with mortals face to face.
Upon the altar next he lays the sapless wood,
While meekly at his side the voiceless victim stood.

But where shall fire be found—extinct the embers lie—
To waft the savour up sweetsmelling to the sky?
The whisper of His child will ever reach His throne,
And bring, as in the Alps, whole avalanches down.
He binds the struggling lamb with awe upon the pile:
" How meek and pure art thou, and man how proud and
    vile."
He said in voiceless words, then sought his brother's face:
" This is a solemn hour, this hill a holy place:
Call now on God the Lord who bids us bring to-day
A sacrifice for sin: stretch forth thy hands and pray."
He lifts his voice in prayer, but raises not his head:
" Eternal Power Unseen! the thing that Thou hast said
This day Thy servants do: if Thou dost ever hear
The voice of seeking man, to us this hour appear!
Behold the offering asked! Accept now from my hand
The thing Thyself hast given, the beauty of the land.
My gift awaits Thy will: do Thou the offering crown
And come, if Thou dost come, with flaming firebrands down."

Dread silence reigns around : no rift is in the cloud,
Meanwhile the younger prays in silence lowly bowed.
Uprising from the earth, he stretches forth his hands,
With face upturned to heaven : meek and devout he stands :
"Great Sovereign of all Worlds, Most Holy Lord of all
Behold us sinful men, who, all unworthy, call
Upon Thy glorious name! not knowing how to ask
The thing we need from Thee : performing this high task
As duty most divine! Hear Lord our helpless cry,
For Thou canst always hear, for Thou art surely nigh
To him who fears Thy name : whose yearning heart is pure
In purpose and desire. Come, if we may endure
Thy Holy Presence, Lord, for we are sinful men :
But Thou didst speak of old—wilt Thou not speak again
With man. Thy servant here, as to Thy child, Thy son !
Speak Thou in mercy Lord or we are all undone :
Great Father of the world : hast Thou not given us birth ?
Then are we sons of God—Thine angels on the earth
Sent forth to live and love : we thirst and pine for Thee !
Not hearing yet we speak ; not seeing ask to see

Thy Holy face of light! Not knowing how to pray
We speak in human words : O send us not away
With barren hearts unblest! For life is one great thirst
For living streams—for Thee! O let the fountains burst
Forth in life's wilderness that we may thirst no more!
Speak as the sighing breeze ; speak as the thunder's roar,
Or speak as never heard, so that Thy Holy voice
But reach our waiting ears, and make these hearts rejoice !
Show us the way of life : show but our gifts approved :
Our offerings lie unsinged, all smokeless, damp, unmoved !
And fire with us is none. O come Eternal Flame
To hallow this dread hour and glorify Thy name !"

Behold the riven cloud ! the sacred fire descends
Bright as the fiery star that oft at eve attends
The paler host of night, or as the lightning flies
When black-browed tempests break across the frowning
    skies.
One altar feels the flame : the living victim bleeds ;
The hissing altar smokes, the flame on fatness feeds.

The fragrant wreaths ascend and mingle with the cloud,
While awe-struck Abel waits rapt, speechless, lowly bowed.
The clouds of morning melt, the radiant sun breaks forth
And gladdens beast and bird in all the smiling earth.
He rises from the ground, and lo, the gifts of Cain
Unasked, unblest, untouched, a withered heap remain!
With steadfast sullen eye he gazes on the stone
Memorial of his sin! and now he stands alone
A marked rejected man, reflecting on his shame.
No fire appeared without: within there springs a flame,
The flame of deadly wrath, the quenchless fire of Hate!
" Is this my recompense! Is this my final fate!"
These were the words he gasped, half-spoken, half-
  suppressed,
And then he went his way, unblessing and unblest.

 The younger owned of God goes forth to meditate
Upon his sacrifice, upon his brother's fate,
Beside his flocks at noon. The day is fair to God,
And very fair to him whose straying footsteps trod

The quiet earth with joy, a joy unknown before.
Henceforth he walks with God while on this mortal shore
With one large pure desire—to do the will of Heaven
And make a Sabbath day of all the sacred seven.
The happy hours steal on in holy reverie :
" O miracle of grace, that God hath answered me
And had respect to me and my meek sacrifice,
And hath redeemed my soul! Is this young lamb the
 price ?
I know not, but He knows : and I will ask no more,
But wait with open ear that from His distant shore
I may some whispers catch, for many voices come.
Methinks, in quiet hours from His cloud-hidden home,
Or where His throne is set. He heard and yet will hear
My prayer and offered praise, for now I feel Him near:
The silence is His home, and all the breathing air
The rustling of His Robe, and time may yet declare
His glory to my sight, if I have eyes to see
Behind this moving Show the Light that shines for me."

So ran his pious thought on that thrice-hallowed day,
Till weary from his joy, in gentle sleep he lay.
Ah, blessed is the sleep that follows duty done,
High duty to our God, and not to man alone !
On such the angels wait and fan with soothing wings,
And mould the dreamy thought that helmless hourly
    springs
Within the helpless mind in sleep's unguarded hour.
For such God's pure still "song" floats down with soothing
    power,
Be it high noon or night, unknown except to them
Who walk with Him by day, who touch His garments hem
With hope in none beside. So was it on that day :
God's silent angels came to teach the " Living Way"
To him who humbly sought and kept the truth he found.

"Hail, faithful child of God ! may light and joy abound,"
The guardian angel said, "For God hath heard thy prayer
And laid thy load on Him who yet shall come to bear

The sin of every man upon his human heart:
Of whom thy lamb was type: and wicked men shall part
The garments of their God, in blind irreverent greed!
But, being offered up, His love shall surely lead
The Kingdoms in his train: for He shall bear the sway
And turn the long black night to everlasting Day.
In Him shall nations hope, and every soul be blest,
And lay upon His Love the troubled soul to rest.
But when He comes to reign, as King from sea to sea
Is hidden in the folds of sacred mystery.

He cometh as a man, though Lord and Judge of all,
To sympathise and serve, and by example call
The erring sons of men from selfishness and pride
To meek all-serving love; He cometh to abide,
As Master, Brother, Friend; no time-bound passing Guest,
In every willing heart: and where He dwells is rest.
He cometh from His throne to seek the strayed and lost
And gather to the fold His flock, a countless host.
With weary feet He'll seek and seek 'until He find'
The furthest straying one, the outcast of mankind.

Beyond the troubled sea of centuries to come
He cometh : lo His word shall strike the ages dumb !
And oft in whispered tones the faithless shall confess
' Of all the sons of men none ever spake like this ! '
His glorious face unseen thou yet shall surely see,
For though unseen, unknown, His love hath ransomed thee."

Thus ends his mortal dream. God's benediction given,
His prostrate body writhes, his spirit soars to Heaven !
For Cain, in jealous wrath, with one fell bloody stroke
Struck out the sacred life ! He slew him ere he woke !
How much a day may hold let this dire day declare:
At morn unbreathing calm: at noon exceeding fair :
The morning heard them pray and saw God's fire descend ;
At noon with deep strange thoughts their wonted way they
    wend :
The same broad sky above. the peaceful earth beneath,
But lo ! the twilight falls upon the face of Death !
And hides a guilty man with all a murderer's woe :
Haste, haste ye brooding shades that unto darkness grow

And hide this horrid sight from beast, from man, from God !
The very beast retires! while ghastly on the sod
A cold stiff body lies, the first fair Godlike form !
Like some proud forest king uprooted by the storm
And withered in the sun ; so lies a brother slain,
With calm uncovered face, exposed to heat and rain !
The halls of Hell resound with wild rejoicings given,
And angels weep to lead the martyr soul to heaven !

 Behold that brooding wretch, whose hand still feels the
  smart
Of that accursed blow that stayed a brother's heart !
No darkness shelters him ! and healing sleep is gone ;
The night is lone and long, but he is not alone !
The night is one great Eye, and many voices come :
His crime cries loud to Heaven, and Heaven speaks back
  his doom.
At midnight forth he creeps to where the murdered lies,
And still the dreadful sight stands bare before his eyes !
He lays a trembling hand upon his brother's head :

"Ah me! 'tis damp and cold: my brother, art thou dead!
Can man the Godlike die as dies the creature slain?
Nay thou art but asleep: awake! No: not again!
For he is cold, dead cold! Nor does he draw one breath
Or my dull ear is stopped: Oh thou art dead! 'tis Death!
Alas that such dread power should lie in this right arm
That never till this day wrought any creature harm!
Twas but one angry blow in thoughtless haste—but one:
How could I work the harm, my brother, but—'tis done!
I tread the earth alone; my roaming parents gone
I know not whither bound: I bear my shame alone!
A double curse I bear, nor hope to be forgiven
For I have slain a man, my brother, friend of Heaven!"

There came an awful Voice from out the deep still night,
And round about him shone a sudden, dazzling light:
"Where is thy brother Abel, whom thy mother bore?
If thou dost well, 'tis well: if ill, then at thy door
Sin lies in wait for thee." To which he made reply:
"I know not: and am I my brother's keeper? I

Who till the ground alone? He slept at setting sun."
The Holy Voice replied: "Go to, what hast thou done?
The voice of human blood, thy brother's blood, now cries
For vengeance from the ground loud clamouring to the skies.
And now accursed art thou from all the fertile land
Which opened wide her mouth for blood hot from thy hand,
Thy brother's blood now shed! When thou dost till the ground
Henceforth it shall not yield her strength, nor fruit abound;
And thou shalt wander wide on earth a fugitive."
"My punishment, how great," he said, "I cannot live!
And bear this crushing curse! And thou hast driven me forth
This day a fugitive, shut out from all the earth!
And from Thy face alas! shut out for evermore!
And all will seek my life: I am afflicted sore!"
The Gracious Voice replied: "Seven times accursed is he
Who takes the life of Cain. I give a sign for thee,
That none may do thee hurt or smite thee in the way."
He waits in hope and fear the dawning of the day.

The rising day has come : he bows his head in prayer,
Then forth to seek the slain : but lo, he is not there !
In night's deep silent hours God's white-robed mourners
    came
To fetch his sacred form and hide this deed of shame.
On noiseless wings they bore to some fair spot unknown
The martyr to his rest, and there they laid him down
In calm unbroken sleep, until that morning break
Deep down within each tomb, when all the dead shall wake,
Uprising at the voice of Him who yet shall come
In glorious majesty to call the nations home.

Sleep on, thou stainless soul : thy grave no eye hath seen,
But nations know thy name and keep thy memory green !
Thy deeds remain untold, thy quiet life unsung ;
They need an angel's pen ! Mine is a mortal tongue,
And mine a sinful hand : but I would fling one flower
Upon the breeze, 'twill find, perchance, thy sacred bower !
Ye winds of heaven waft on this poor unopened bud,
And bear it to that bower where sleeps the friend of God !

PRIZE ELEGY:
To a Welshman.

Thine earthly form mine eyes have never seen
   Yet may I call thee human brother, friend ;
For dearer friends on earth have never been
   Than those who seek His welcome at the end.

Alone they travel up the self-same hill
   With one high purpose—pressing on to God,
With sigh and song they journey hoping still
   Till each poor pilgrim gains His blest abode.

In other lands thy pious fathers lie
   Perchance some hoary mountain guards the place,
Some village Bethel haply watches by,
   Some crumbling stone whose words we cannot trace.

A distant shore thy wandering footsteps trod
   Thy native hills with grief were left behind
Thy body sleeps beneath the Southern sod
   And o'er it moans the gentle Southern wind.

THE LIGHT OF EDEN.

But God shall watch their sleeping dust and thine.
    His joy of old was with the sons of men,
And where His holy dead in peace recline
    His voice shall come and call them forth again.

How sad his lot who never knew a friend,
    Who restless round the heartless world doth roam,
Whose wants in death no loving hands attend,
    For whom the grave alone affords a home!

But smoother was thy pathway, brother gone;
    Affection's beam shone ever on thy way;
Thy griefs and burdens were not borne alone
    For God and loved ones cheered the saddest day.

And love though human is not born of earth,
    The love of children and the widowed heart;
Ah, surely these are of celestial birth
    And those who love nor life nor death can part.

Ah! vacant home where brooding sorrow flings
    A gloom and sadness rudely over all!
The angels bore him on their shining wings
    And left instead black Sorrow's blackest pall!

PRIZE ELEGY: TO A WELSHMAN.

Nay, read not thus the doings of His love,
  The daylight hides the stars from mortal eye ;
Oft in the night from God's bright heaven above
  The guardian angels come and hover nigh.

Ye lonely hearts that crushed and broken mourn
  Your loved one is not bound within the tomb !
He surely lives, to Heaven's bright mansions borne,
  Where death is not and vanished is the gloom.

God's healing Hand be on your stricken head
  To soothe and comfort all the weary way,
And, through the night, His angels round your bed
  To make its darkness radiant as the day.

His holy word proclaims Him ever near
  The widow's Helper and the children's Friend ;
His gentle word can dry the bitter tear
  And cheer you daily to the journey's end.

The tuneful voice that led the holy hymn
  No longer thrills us in the house of prayer :
But memory holds some echoes faint and dim
  Like distant strains borne on the evening air.

But there are choirs that gather round the throne
   Where ransomed voices raise the glad " new song : "
And with what joy he'll learn that song unknown
   And wear the vesture of that shining throng !

Ah. heaven at last ! no weary parting more :
   For him the joy, the vision of the blest :
For us the strife upon this mortal shore
   Until He calls us to His promised rest.

SOMETHING FAR AWAY.

What means, my heart, this sad unrestful longing
   This constant grasping at the dim unknown ?
Is there no rest, no Heaven in daily duty.
   In things at hand which thou mayst call thine own ?

Tis not the woods in leafy mantles folded.
   At dewy morn or at the close of day,
That float before me like a captive's vision :
   'Tis only something somewhere far away.

'Tis not by tarns nursed in the lap of mountains
   In loneliness my wandering feet would stray;
Nor where I roamed in days of happy childhood;
   'Tis only somewhere seeming far away.

'Tis not beyond the wide unresting ocean,
   Where loved ones name me when they kneel to pray;
My spirit longs like some lost child aweary
   For something or for some one far away.

'Tis not for crowds that surge in sleepless cities
   Where night is restless as the common day;
Ah no! of these my heart is often weary
   And longs for something somewhere far away.

'Tis not for tones of voices from the Silence
   And forms that vanished as the light of day;
No poet's dream hath given it form or being,
   And yet it must be somewhere far away.

'Tis not for strains of Earth's divinest music,
   The distant echoes of some holy lay
That come at times from out the deep Eternal;
   Ah no! 'tis only something far away.

It may be Love, a blind and voiceless passion,
  Too shy to face the common light of day;
It may be so: I only know 'tis something
  That hovers formless ever far away.

Perchance 'tis Heaven that opens to my spirit,
  Or angel whispers, mystic dreams of day;
I only know 'tis not an empty phantom
  But something real—only far away.

IN MEMORIAM:

To my Sunday=School Teacher.

And must I think thee dead, my friend?
  The stalwart body lying still,
  And paralysed the potent will?
Of all these powers is this the end?

IN MEMORIAM: TO MY SUNDAY SCHOOL TEACHER.

I thought thee heir to length of days :
    Thy well-built frame seemed to defy
    All mortal darts : but dangers lie
In smooth as well as rugged ways.

This world is one vast burying place,
    We live as neighbours with the dead :
    In moss-grown graveyards perhaps we tread
Upon our great grandfather's face,

As 'neath the yew tree's spreading boughs,
    That shade the entrance to the shrine
    Where, in the threefold name Divine
Our parents made their marriage vows,

We stand, and one with reverence reads
    The faded letters on the stone,
    And in a still more serious tone
The verse that tells of noble deeds.

Our ancestors are lying here
    Whose faces we have never seen ;
    But as we read what they have been
Emotion stirs the hidden tear.

We wonder if our faces bear
    Some likeness to these faded ones,
    And as our fancy backward runs
We wonder like to whom they were.

We think of eyes that oft have gazed
    Upon the old familiar tree,
    And things like these which now we see—
Green graves, old stones, and names erased;

And wonder which of us could boast,
    Could we behold the first that lay
    Where generations sleep to-day,
" 'Tis I resemble him the most!"

We think of men of stalwart frame
    Who shunned the straw-thatched village inn,
    Came to the church, confessed their sin,
And then returned the way they came,

Or with the village preacher walked
    Across the green, and o'er the moor,
    And meeting either rich or poor
They stopped, and all like brothers talked

We think of boys sat on the grass
   Who shyly rise from where they sat,
   And each one doffs his Sunday hat
As on their way these good men pass.

And musing thus we seem to stand
   Linked with the living and the dead :
   The parting line seems but a thread,
And yet it is an iron band.

We cannot see the stately form,
   Though only on the other side :
   The line seems now an ocean wide,
And on it rides the sweeping storm.

We cannot see the face we loved—
   We love it still where'er it be—
   We cannot solve the mystery,
It may be near or far removed.

The friendly voice we cannot hear,
   Its earthly song has died away :
   We trust he chants a holier lay
In tones too pure for mortal ear.

We trust the note on which he sings
   Comes from the everlasting lyre,
   To which the great seraphic choir
Call out the fulness of their strings.

But fancy seems again to wake
   The faded echoes of the past,
   And each one, fainter than the last.
A wider circle seems to make.

And softly on the soul it falls
   As far away it gently dies,
   Like distant organ peals that rise
And steal without the sacred walls.

Imagination strives to soar
   Above the sky, beyond the grave;
   But all is as the boundless wave,
An ocean dark without a shore.

The wonders wrapped within the veil
   The restless fancy fondly paints;
   But, soaring daily, sad, it faints,
And only tries again to fail.

IN MEMORIAM: TO MY SUNDAY SCHOOL TEACHER.

The vision passes like the wind
   That wrecks the vessel on the main,
   It stamps no image on the brain.
Nor leaves a vestige in the mind.

What now the opened eyes behold
   'Twere impious to attempt to say :
   The trials of Life's little day
May now their mystery unfold.

The goodness of the seeming ill
   May open on the wandering soul,
   For Death, we think, is not the goal,
But knowledge marches onward still.

So Nature's book would have us think—
   And in another Book we find
   Hints of a chain we call the mind,
Of which this life is but a link.

We cling to Life through every stage
   With all the power that Life can give :
   Man's strongest passion is " to live,"
Nor does it leave him in old age.

The world may show a frowning face,
    And daily hardships be his lot :
    His home may be a cheerless cot,
And yet he connot quit the " race."

Tis sweet to live although it mean
    An unavailing fight with death,
    Which makes him sigh with every breath,
" 'Twere better never to have been."

The suicidal mind that wreaks
    Its frenzy on the outward frame,
    And closes thus a life of shame,
Declares it is not Death it seeks,

But life without the shame and pain :
    It loves not Death for Death's own sake,
    But as from sleep it hopes to wake,
And feel that death has been a gain.

The swallows twittering o'er the grave
    Where now my old companion lies
    At Instinct's bidding upward rise,
And wing their way across the wave.

IN MEMORIAM: TO MY SUNDAY SCHOOL TEACHER. 87

They know not why nor where they go,
   But faithful Instinct leads aright,
   Nor leaves them in their pathless flight
To where the milder breezes blow.

The human Spirit longs to fly,
   And faithful Instinct seems to say,
   "There is a Life beyond to-day,"
And Instinct never tells a lie.

In Reason's unmolested hours,
   When Fear has turned its ghostly face,
   And Faith assumes her proper place,
We dread not Death's destructive powers.

We sometimes fear that Life may be
   Confined to "three-score years and ten;"
   But something in the souls of men
Seems grasping at Eternity.

The swallow is not led astray
   When prompted by the Greater Mind
   To leave its mud-walled house behind,
And seek awhile a sunnier day.

There is a distant sunny land
   To which instinctively it flies :
   It finds the clime of cloudless skies,
Led by the Great Unerring Hand.

And so the passion in the soul,
   That ever pants for endless life,
   And prompts it to the fiercest strife,
With what we sometimes deem the goal

Of all, is but the "still small voice"
   In tones too low for Reason's ear ;
   But blessed are the souls that hear,
And, hearing, worship and rejoice.

It bids us think of other hills
   Where mortal feet have never stood,
   The home of God and all the good,
The refuge from all human ills.

And when this little day is past,
   With all its gladness and its grief,
   The Hope, now preaching firm belief,
Will not play truant at the last.

IN MEMORIAM: TO MY SUNDAY SCHOOL TEACHER.

If in the soul there lives a Force
    That makes it crave at every stage
    A life that will not bend with age,
When suns shall totter from their course,

'Tis not a fancy straying wild,
    A phantom leading Thought astray,
    'Tis Nature pointing out the way,
And Nature never mocks her child.

We sometimes call this life a " dream "—
    It may be truer than we think :
    For when we reach the dreaded brink,
And step into the chilling stream,

We may with suddenness awake
    To see what purer eyes have seen :
    To see how fruitless life has been,
And deeply mourn the great mistake.

The truth may dawn upon us then,
    Which we before refused to see—
    That what affects man's destiny
Should be the foremost thought with men :

That wealth and fame are not the whole
  That should engross the active brain :
  There is for man a greater gain,
There is a fortune for the soul.

I sing this sad and broken lay
  To thee, the friend of days gone bye :
  And as I sing I heave a sigh,
And think of that maturer day

When new ambitions filled my mind,
  And led me from the haunts of youth
  To where I learned the sterner truth,
That friends like thee were hard to find.

The happy days and weeks we spent,
  Though covered by eventful years,
  Spring forth from memory, just as tears
Oft follow some far off event.

I seem to see the furrowed soil,
  Where thou did sow the pregnant grain,
  And watch with thee the kindly rain
That came to bless thy honest toil.

Again I hear the lowing herd
   That sought the grass of early spring;
   Again I hear the blackbird sing.
And many a little chirping bird.

Once more I tread th' aspiring blade
   Beneath the over-hanging trees:
   Once more I breathe the fragrant breeze
That fanned the leaflets in the glade.

The murmur of the limpid brook
   Seems now to gather in my ear:
   While memory paints the little weir
That we constructed in the nook.

The playful lamb again I see
   That gamboled on the ancient mound,
   And others stretched upon the ground,
And others grazing on the lea.

And then the sunny summer day
   Springs forth, like thy familiar smile.
   And by the awkward wooden stile
I seem to smell the new-mown hay.

Strong men with busy hands are there,
    And thou the stateliest of them all,
    Fit rival for the Hebrew Saul,
And soon the fertile field is bare.

I think of climbing up the hill,
    When dewdrops sparkled on the ground,
    And on the ear there fell no sound
Except the murmur of the rill.

The sweetness of the tranquil morn
    Seems yet to linger in my soul;
    I feel the rustling breeze that stole
Across the fields of ripening corn.

The farmstead nestling in the wood
    Lives like a picture in my mind;
    Again I hear the angry wind,
And see the spot where oft I stood;

Once more I hear the tempest howl
    Amid the tall and silvery firs;
    Once more I hear the yelping curs,
Roused by the hooting of the owl.

And other thoughts and other things
 Are wakened when I hear thy name.
 But nothing is to me the same.
For Death o'er all a shadow flings.

I mourn thee not as others may—
 A cheerful neighbour, quick to lend
 The aid and counsel of a friend.
And by example sketch the way.

I mourn thee as my guide in youth,
 Whose influence formed my plastic mind.
 And pointed where the soul may find
The germ, if not the flower of Truth.

To me not merely bosom friend,
 Nor elder brother—this were much ;
 But more a father, and as such
Thou didst the fatherless defend.

Would that my Muse could sing thy worth
 In words more eloquent and wise :
 I fain would write upon the skies
The name that may not live on earth.

But better far than honest praise
  Is to have merited the same;
  If those have cause to bless our name
With whom we spent our little days,

We shall not then have lived in vain.
  And though no stone should mark the place
  Where we shall close this earthly race
A deathless influence will remain.

There is a better monument
  Than earth's best sculptor ever wrought:
  'Tis not of stone, 'twas never bought—
The memory of a life well spent.

Thy name (and mine) may be unknown
  Ere half a century shall have past;
  But deeds of virtue still will last
When Time shall wreck the costliest stone.

Let it be mine to follow thee
  In every holy work and word,
  As thou didst follow where thy Lord
Had marked the way for thee and me.

IN MEMORIAM: TO MY SUNDAY SCHOOL TEACHER.

Thy life is fairer in my sight
    Since thou hast reached the mystic goal,
    And deeper passion fills my soul
That I may reach an equal height

In every pure and noble aim.
    Thy "eventide" was "light" indeed :
    Thy sunbeams closed with rapid speed,
Yet brilliant were the last that came.

Far from the babble and the strife
    That in life's great arenas swell
    Content thou wast *unknown* to dwell
Through all the stages of thy life.

The limpid streamlet dashing down
    The cascades of its native hill
    Turns cheerfully the village mill
Before it babbles through the town.

It laves the daisy's golden eye
    That opens near its splashing spray.
    As well as kissing on its way
The flowers that charm each passer-by.

It bathes the leaflets, as it falls
   From rock to rock in wooded glen :
   And seems as pure and proud as when
It laves some ancient castle walls.

'Tis not the broad and turbid stream
   Where boats and barges daily ply
   That charms the meditative eye
Or lures the poet in a dream :

The murmur of the babbling brook
   Is sweeter than the splash of oars :
   And, where the foaming cascade roars,
Or in the weird, umbrageous nook

He finds the key to purest song,
   And so, my brother, thou didst find
   Thy music in the changing wind,
Far from th' excitement-seeking throng.

But as I sing I half forget
   That thou hast left thy well-kept farm :
   The life has left thy powerful arm,
Thy brow is damp with icy sweat.

IN MEMORIAM: TO MY SUNDAY SCHOOL TEACHER.

Thy eye has shed its latest tear,
    Thy hand has lost its wonted skill ;
    Thy warm and faithful heart is still,
Thy soul—gone to another sphere.

Yes, friends have laid thee 'neath the sod,
    Thy body sleeps among the dead ;
    Thy ransomed spirit now has fled,
And lives in perfect peace with God.

And loving ones are left behind
    To mourn a father or a friend ;
    And with their sighs my sigh shall blend.
For thou to me wast ever kind ;

And as I think of all thy worth,
    Thy patience in the trying hour ;
    I'll trust, like thee, the Higher Power,
And walk towards Heaven while here on earth.

THE UNIVERSAL CREED.

Why mourn we so the forward van
   The leaders into life
Who follow where the soul of man
   Doth rest from mortal strife?
The mighty spirits all have said:
" The dear departed are not dead."

The petals from the flower may fall,
   The blossoms fade away,
The stem and branches wither—all,
   In sombre sad decay:
Yet priests of Nature oft have said:
" The dear departed are not dead."

The heart is riven with sudden grief,
   The scalding teardrops come,
The nights, the noons, bring no relief,
   A shadow clouds the home!
Though Priest and Prophet ever said:
" The dear departed are not dead."

THE UNIVERSAL CREED.

O solemn Death! dread Mystery!
   Thy shadow chills the spheres
The fruitless Past the fair To Be
   Are heirs to blood and tears!
Still human hope has ever said :
"The dear departed are not dead."

Dear pensive souls that wander far
   In fields of troubled thought
If spirits live in every star
   Think ye they sorrow not?
Rest troubled heart : His saints have said :
"The dear departed are not dead?"

Yea, wait in hope each soul of man,
   Let Goodness be thy goal,
Though life be here a fevered span
   A pruning of the soul,
Nurse in thy heart what Jesus said :
"The dear departed are not dead."

IN MEMORIAM.
Rev. J. F. Ewing, M.A.

Strong manly son of Scotia wild—
   We mourn thee, sweet transparent soul,
   Life's massive fragment, not the whole :
We mourn thee, Nature's noble child.

We mourn thee, faithful shepherd gone :
   Thy day was filled with earnest toil,
   That nought thy growing flock might spoil.
Nor ill o'ertake some straying one.

A leader lost we mourn to-day,
   A cultured spirit, brave and wise,
   Whose clearer vision helped our eyes
To see the landmarks of the way.

The changing Thought, the changeless Truth,
   The wider outlook of the time,
   The freer Faith, intact, sublime
He knew, and preached to baffled youth.

The voice that warned of rock and reef,
   The words that left his fervid tongue,
   That cheered the old and charmed the young,
The smile that brightened brooding grief,

These all are gone! We ask not why:
   Be ours the Faith that folds her wings
   When search is done, and calmly sings
" I shall not altogether die."

Peace to the land that gave thee birth,
   The land where all thy fathers sleep,
   The land where now thy loved ones weep,
The home of learning, reverence, worth.

And peace to you, poor widowed hearts,
   His dearest in this " vale of tears."
   God comfort her—bowed down with years—
Whose twice-bewidowed spirit smarts.

And her—bereft of all most dear—
   God comfort her, all comfortless;
   And light with hope her dark distress,
And wipe away her bitter tear!

A noble friendship fitly ends:
  The old companions meet once more:
  What welcome to our southern shore,
What joy for them, devoted friends!

But scarce within the sacred spot,
  When one is smitten, tended, lost!
  Behold the dear, delighted host
Extends his welcome, then—" is not."

The dearest one is o'er the sea
  To bless a mother's even tide:
  But, to the last, there stands beside
That dying bed—Fidelity.

WILD FLOWERS.
(Lines Addressed to a Lover of Flowers).

As pure as the angels of light,
  And like them God's messengers, too:
Ah, surely these flowerets so bright
  Have a message for me and for you.

Their faces look up to the sky,
    Yet they scatter their odours on earth.
And this for the soul's inner eye
    Is a vision of infinite worth.

They smile on the high and the low,
    They beautify mountain and vale,
Thus causing His children to know
    That *nowhere* His goodness shall fail.

They bloom in the forest's deep shade—
    Fair Temple of God undefiled :
They gladden the glen and the glade,
    And speak to the sage and the child.

They speak to the heart that is pure
    Of the Pure One who watches o'er all :
Of a Love that will ever endure
    And care for the great and the small.

WINTER : A SONG.

(*Music by Mr. W. Hodgett*).

Oh, weary hours of winter drear
   How deep the gloom that covers all !
No flower adorns the hemisphere—
   Death folds us in his sable pall :
The lark is still, the swallow fled,
   The fields are brown, the trees are bare :
Hope on, my soul ! they are not dead,
   They sweetly sleep in Nature's care.

The winds are cold and hoarsely moan,
   The storm is sweeping o'er the moor ;
O'er Nature's face a veil is thrown—
   The snowdrift blocks my cottage door :
The frost has nipped each tender blade.
   Is not this world a " vale of tears ? "
Hope on, my heart ! be not dismayed
   The snowdrop's head again appears !

WINTER: A SONG.

The earth is dead and icy cold :
   I walk 'midst relics of the past :
The years fly on, I'm growing old
   A few more days and then—the last !
The Spring of Life, how fast it flies,
   And wintry age brings myriad pains :
Hope on, my soul ! thou yet shalt rise
   And live where Spring immortal reigns !

SATURDAY EVENING :
A Sonnet.

The six days' toil again have passed away :
   How swift the silent moments roll
   Into the past ! But thou, my soul,
Art destined to behold that day—
The time of which no creature tongue can say —
   When heaven's loud-sounding bell shall toll,
   And earth, ablaze from pole to pole,
Shall God's unchanging plan display,

And ransomed souls, from Zion's peaceful height—
The faithful who have gone before—
With steady gaze shall see the wondrous sight
From far, and hear that sentence swore,
When God shall send His messenger of light
To swear that time shall be no more!

SWEET FLOWERS OF SPRING.

(Written for Nottingham May Festival, 1888.

Music by Mr. W. Hodgett.

Sweet is the dawn, Spring's dawn of gladness,
Dispersing gloom and soothing sadness,
Fair flowers shall charm Earth's fevered madness
    And on the breeze sweet odours fling :
The lark is gay, for day is breaking,
And Winter's night the earth forsaking,
And for its tomb soft showers are making
    A wreath of flowers, sweet flowers of Spring.

On mountain slopes, where streams are rushing
From hoary rocks and fountains gushing,
The lonely flower is meekly blushing—
    Though born of earth, a saintly thing :
No human hand with touch defiling
Has placed it there where, daily smiling,
And every beast and bird beguiling,
    Its modest grace adorns the Spring.

In smiling vales the South wind sighing
Wakes myriad buds in beauty vieing,
While, veiled in grass, serenely lying
    To Nature's breast bright daisies cling :
The primrose from the brake is peeping,
And sparkling dew each flower is steeping,
For Flora fair her charge is keeping
    With dewy hand, to deck the Spring.

Come welcome flowers with dewdrops bending,
O'er hill and dell sweet fragrance sending,
And to the world a glory lending
    Which nought beside can ever bring :

For you, fair flowers, my heart is yearning,
With hope and fear my breast is burning;
Begone, dull care! for lo, returning,
    Again I see sweet flowers of Spring!

THE SWALLOW.

Welcome, welcome twittering swallow,
    On my housetop rest thy wing;
Verdant fields and blossoms follow
    Where thou comest, queen of Spring.

Deny my thatch to thee? No, never!
    Thou art always welcome there;
With delight thou fill'st me ever
    As thou flittest through the air.

Oft I think I hear thee singing
    Of another far-off home,
As aloft I see thee winging
    High above yon sacred dome.

Tender broods their wings are trimming
  Soon to leave our country dear,
Others o'er the brook are skimming
  Kissing soft its waters clear.

As away I see thee flying
  O'er the ocean's silvery foam,
To my soul a voice seems crying :
  "Child! this world is not thy home."

" Learn a lesson from the swallow
  Like thyself a pilgrim here :
Winter storms fair Spring must follow
  When thou, too, must disappear."

THE ROSE IN THE WOOD.

A lonely pathway through the wood
  Led to the village school,
And there when summer's sun was high
  'Twas always fresh and cool.

And when returning oft I've sat
   And listened to the birds,
Whose blithful song in vain I try
   To tell to you in words.

One day appeared a tiny rose ;
   'Twas bending 'neath the dew.
Exhaling such a pleasant smell,
   Of such a charming hue !

I called to see it every day,
   Delighted with my gem :
But ever downward hung its head,
   So fragile was its stem.

One night a thunderstorm arose,
   The lightning blazed amain,
The sky was black, the thunder roared,
   In torrents fell the rain !

Next morning all was calm and bright,
   The storm had passed away ;
But oh ! that tender little rose
   Across the pathway lay !

THE ROSE IN THE WOOD.

The rain had broke its slender stem,
    Its comeliness had fled,
And 'neath the sun's fierce scorching rays
    Lay low its withered head.

The trees seemed weeping all around
    Like tears the raindrops stood,
And all the breezes murmured o'er
    The rose of that lone wood.

Then spake the spirit of the wood,
    Calm as when angels pray :
" Frail mortal, thou art, like that rose,
    A creature of a day."

Grieve not, my heart : do thou but shed
    The fragrance God has given :
Smile undisturbed, nor fear the night,
    'Tis but the dawn of Heaven !

SPRING.

Time's steady wheel has turned again
    To earth a fairer garb to give;
And hill and dell and smiling plain
    All sing for joy. "Behold we live!"

The sun has shot a milder ray
    Across the hoary-headed hills,
And chased stern Winter's corse away—
    No more his lifeless shadow chills.

A breeze from Eden's unknown grave
    Has breathed across the dreary wild,
A vernal gleam has crossed the wave
    And on the wreck of Winter smiled.

The dove has sped o'er waters dark
    To view the devastated scene :
The dove of Spring has moored her barque
    With cargo of ambrosial green.

SPRING.

O Spring, transformer of the globe,
    Would that thou didst perennial reign !
That thou wouldst spoil grim Winter's robe
    And bind the monster with thy chain !

Would that with thy celestial wand
    Thou wouldst this planet rule for aye,
And bind the seasons in thy bond
    And thou alone the sceptre sway !

By rippling rills and murmuring brooks
    The seasons' queen has lately passed,
On highway sides and hidden nooks
    Her smile benignant she has cast.

The mountain torrent's frantic waves
    Have kissed her leafy garment's hem ;
The rolling river gently laves
    The flower she poised on fragile stem.

Fair Spring, what beauty comes with thee !
    What pleasures follow in thy train !
Soft zephyrs from the heaving sea,
    And copious showers of gentle rain.

Thou art in fairer vestments dressed
    Than monarch's bride on festal morn,
No foreign beauties deck thy breast—
    Thy beauty all was with thee born.

The crown that glitters on thy head
    Hath gems to scatter everywhere;
Some mark the spot where sleep the dead
    Some sparkle by the lion's lair.

Glad Spring, that scatteres' sunbeams bright,
    And showers refreshing hill and dale;
Thy smile regales my inner sight,
    I read with joy thy sacred tale.

The lessons in thy sparkling dew,
    The sermons in thy blushing flowers
Though ever old, are ever new,
    And furnish thought for quiet hours.

Thou speakest of sublimest things:
    Of life, of death, of something more—
That man's immortal soul hath wings
    To waft him to a happier shore!

Through seeming death a spark of life
   Shoots upward 'neath thy magic ray,
And where the monster Death seemed rife
   'Tis Life that holds the sovereign sway.

O Spring! O Life! O soul of mine!
   How will ye in that day compare?
Wilt thou, my soul, arise to shine
   Or droop and die in dark despair?

THE SHEPHERD OF RADNOR FOREST.

The storm-beaten brow of the mountain I see,
   As my fathers have seen it before,
But where is the oak, that stately old tree,
   That adorned it in summers of yore?

The warblers are mute and the forest is shorn
   By the scathing mutations of years;
Now climbing the rock a stunted old thorn
   Like a weatherworn pilgrim appears.

The wolf and the stag have long vanished from view.
    Reynard only now there may abide :
And age after age the lamb and the ewe—
    Harmless creatures—have grazed on its side.

The breezes' soft sigh there for ages hath tried
    To outrival the streamlet's faint moan :
But morning's great orb this conflict espied
    And declared that the meed was his own.

When o'er the bald heights golden javelins were hurled
    Soon dispersing the fog from the plain
The shepherd looked down and smiled on the world
    Where assiduously labored the swain.

Then slowly he wends down the hillside so steep,
    To the homestead he now must return.
And starts as a hare affrighteth the sheep
    As it bounds through the dew-laden fern.

And while the bright sun blazing on through the skies,
    Drinks the dewdrops that shine on the lea
A stranger to care in slumber he lies
    'Neath the shade of a sycamore tree.

THE SHEPHERD OF RADNOR FOREST.

When zephyrs grow cool and the last rays of gold
   Gently linger awhile in the west,
He climbs the steep hill to visit the fold
   Where the sheep must be gathered to rest.

I look to the hill as in boyhood's bright morn
   When a stranger to sorrow and care,
And sheep as of old its bald summit adorn
   But the shepherd, where is he? ah! where?

In safety gone home to the sheep-fold above,
   Where the wolf is forever unknown;
The Shepherd of all with tenderest love
   Kindly took him, and called him His own.

That Shepherd still lives, happy thought for the sheep,
   Where the pastures for ever shall bloom,
And every dear lamb He offers to keep,
   For in heaven there is plenty of room.

Ye scenes of my youth, how I long for you now
   As I roam on this fair southern strand!
Ye still are the same, but lo, on my brow
   Time is writing with merciless hand!

CAMBRIA:
A Song.

Dear land of dauntless chief and warrior,
   Lift up with pride thy cloud-wreathed head :
Ye winds blow soft o'er hill and hamlet,
   Lest ye awake her stainless dead !
O Cambria, Cambria, the land that gave me birth,
Thou art, wild Wales, with hills and dales,
The dearest spot on all the earth !

Dear land of hoary bard and minstrel
   Thy garland has not faded yet ;
I bless thy song and harp Æolian
   And pray thy sun may never set !
O Cambria, Cambria, the land that gave me birth,
Thou art to me, thou fair and free,
The dearest spot on all the earth !

Dear land of weird enraptured preacher,
    Thy sons have thrilled the sons of men ;
And from thy hills and lonely valleys
    The great Chrysostoms come again !
O Cambria, Cambria, the land that gave me birth,
Long wilt thou be, dear land to me,
The dearest spot on all the earth !

Fair land of soft, abiding beauty,
    O'er peaceful glens thy castles frown :
Sleep, sleep in peace, ye glorious Glyndwrs,
    Henceforth be peace thy chief renown !
O Cambria, Cambria, the land that gave me birth,
From o'er the sea I turn to thee,
Thou dearest spot on all the earth !

A SHOOTING STAR:

A Sonnet.

Ere down to rest I laid my weary head
Into the spangled vault I gazed afar,
And in the boundless wild beheld a star
Most bright: when, lo! it like a meteor fled
Swift as the lightning through the heavens it sped
Down towards the sunset like a flaming car
As if in haste the helpless globe to mar,
Or on mankind a greater light to shed.
To mortal eye it aimless seemed to roll
Unguided through the great sidereal realm
Where countless orbs that all our thought o'erwhelm
Stood undisturbed. Not so: He doth control
Erratic stars. Then will He leave my soul
To steer her barque with no one at the helm?

THE AUSTRALIAN BLACK.

Wild son of fair Australia's plains
I sing in no unfeeling strains
Thy waning hopes, thy growing pains,
 For art thou not my brother?
A savage heart beats in thy breast
But ah, thy lot has been unblest!
Yet still thine ebon arms have pressed
 A human form—a mother.

In other days behold him roam,
The boundless " bush," his happy home,
And o'er his head Heaven's arching dome
 A king in every feature!
But now, O shame! behold him come
From out his ancient groves of gum
To cringe and beg for beer or rum
 A blighted, ruined creature!

His placid lakes with sable swan,
Where generations ages gone
Found food and sport for sire and son,
   Dread White-men haunt and plunder:
They fell and spoil his ancient trees
That bore a whole millennium's breeze ;
They hew and hack where'er they please
   And cleave his woods asunder.

Beneath that tangled roof of hair
There hides a brow unmarked with care
And from within fierce eyeballs glare—
   He heeds no forest barrier :
Behold him hurl his wooden spear !
Within his breast there dwells no fear,
But, free, he roves from year to year
   A stout and skillful warrior.

With skill he throws his boomerang;
Lo, in his hut strange weapons hang!
Alas, that poet never sang
   His thousand deeds of slaughter!
With skins and feathers see him drest,
For love has touched his human breast :
There's one more comely than the rest
   And she's the chieftain's daughter!

His words lived only on his tongue,
His songs are lost, his harp unstrung,
His deeds of daring die unsung
   From countless generations.
Perchance he had his Iliad too,
Now vanished as the morning dew :
His deeds and he pass from our view—
   Alas for Christain nations!

THE LIGHT OF EDEN.

The curse of Cain lies on our head,
And now his race will soon be dead
We send him clothes and give him bread,
   But first we gave him brandy!
We landed on his native shore
And drove him rudely from our door,
And where he reigned a King of yore
   Now struts the British dandy!

And were not life and country dear
To him who owned a hemisphere?
Poor Black, I'll drop one honest tear,
   My heart can do no other!
No more thy wild corroboree,
No more thy ancient dynasty,
And who shall write thy history,
   Thou hapless human brother?

AN AUSTRALIAN NATIONAL SONG.

Stand up Australians bold !
Be brave in deed and word.
    Then no alarm shall work us harm
    While one right arm
Can strike a blow or wield a sword !

    Chorus : Then let the dingo howl,
        Our King's the Kangaroo ;
        No beast of prey shall hold the sway
        Or us dismay
        While young Australia's heart is true !

Roll on, old ocean roll
Around our Southern shore,
    Thy harbours fair and bracing air
    Shall banish care
And wed us to thee evermore !

We love our brother man,
But keep your hands away,
 For hand to hand we'll ever stand
 And guard this land
Or die the bravest of the day!

We fear no foreign foe,
We give each man his share :
 But tyrants old from countries cold
 Don't be too bold
Sleep on within your ancient lair!

WAITING THE EVENTIDE.

Ye evening shades fall gently down
 And hide the busy scenes of earth :
Come, tranquil hour, Night's sombre crown,
 Earth's sweetest balm its daily birth.

WAITING THE EVENTIDE.

Come welcome rest, nor stay thy flight,
   And o'er us spread thy noiseless wing :
We hail thy advent, peaceful night,
   When Nature's silent songsters sing.

Unroll thy mantle, queen of peace,
   And veil from view those scenes of care ;
'Tis thine from toil to give release
   And drown the cries that rend the air.

Thy silent coming glad we see
   As o'er the hills thy form steals on :
Spread o'er us soon thy canopy,
   And bid the toils of day begone.

Yea, speed o'er earth thy chariot dark
   Thou shadow of a better rest :
And hide all but devotion's spark,
   That spark that lights the human breast.

EARLY MORNING PRAYER.
Ps. v. 3.

Hear from the distant ages a sentiment sublime,
Unchanged by falling empires, untouched by blighting Time.
In tones of solemn sweetness upon the ear it rings
Like echoes of the music from David's sacred strings.
Sweet harp! I think I hear it as struck by one of old
When these sweet words of David my wondering eyes behold :
" My voice in early morning O Lord to Thee shall rise,
My prayer shall be directed to Thee above the skies : "
His noble heart is throbbing with anguish for his son
Fatigued in mind and body, the vital force is done
Until renewed by slumber, refresher of mankind,
Best refuge for the weary and cordial for the mind.
He lays him down nor utters a prayer of wonted length
When Nature's flickering embers have lost their native
  strength.

But, knowing that Jehovah his secret thought can see,
He cries: " In early morning, my prayer shall rise to Thee."
No sleepy words are muttered: a sigh to him is prayer:
But when refreshed by slumber and morning's fragrant air
His voice rings out in praises; for all is calm and bright,
And hill and dell are smiling to welcome morning light.
Sweet morn! whose haunted stillness no human voice doth
    break
But Nature's thousand voices their matchless music wake:
How sweet to climb the mountain in these pacific hours,
When fragrant breezes rustle amid the lonely flowers,
And view the sleeping hill-tops and verdant peaceful vale
Where flowers in modest beauty their fragrant streams
    exhale!
How lovely now the meadows, how pure the sparkling rill!
How fair the golden sunbeams just peeping o'er the hill!
How charming too the forest in morning's peaceful dawn
Where frantic in the shadows parade the bounding fawn!
O pleasant tranquil morning! when all earth's toilers rest,
Before earth's burning problems excite the fevered breast,

Thou art, indeed, an emblem of Heaven's exhaustless cup
At whose o'erflowing splashes the thirsty soul may sup.
How sweet to praise our Maker at this delightful time
When all His vast creation makes melody sublime!
When all earth's din and discord is silent as the grave,
What laughter in the streamlet, what music in the wave!
What heavenly thoughts are floating upon the morning breeze,
What visions in the dewdrops, what voices in the trees!
O David, thou didst wisely prefer the morning air
To waft beyond these shadows thy wants to God in prayer!
A landscape fair as Eden would meet the quickened gaze,
The Spirit's noonday splendours upon the soul would blaze:
The breezes from Mount Zion and Heaven's refreshing dew
Would fill the soul with music and string his harp anew.
Then in the early morning my prayer shall soar on high
When all things chant His praises in earth and sea and sky.

ODE TO A BIRTHDAY.

Come, welcome day! I'll greet thy dawn
    Let cloud or sunshine thee attend ;
If glistening dewdrops deck the lawn
    And make the feebler flowerets bend.

Or flaming Phœbus loose the band
    That binds the daisy's golden eye
Unbolting with his magic hand
    The flood-gates where all odours lie.

Howe'er thou come this eye of mine
    Will see thee lovlier than thy peers,
For thou—accept the honour thine—
    Dost mark the measure of her years :—

The years of her whose life and love
    Have cheered and blessed another life
Come then as peaceful as the dove,
    Or come with threatening omens rife,

Thou canst not rob this happy heart
 Of joys which dates not day-breaks bring ;
Still thou mayst play a welcome part
 And o'er the date thy blessing fling.

Still may the life whose added years
 Give thee thy charm and prompt this rhyme,
Or crowned with joy or calmed with tears
 Be guarded by the King of Time.

TO EVE'S FAIREST DAUGHTER.

Is it a face from the realms on high ?
It must have been cast in a heavenly die
 For it beams with ineffable grace ;
The light that shoots from that radiant eye
It fills my soul ! Yet I can but *sigh*
 For the form that I may not *embrace*.

That heart may be dead to the magic power
That *this* may feel in the opening flower
 That blooms by the murmuring rill :
One palate may be so morbidly sour
As to drink unmoved of the nectar shower,
 The Elysian fair arbours distil.

One eye may gaze on the heavens at night,
And feel no thrill at the wondrous sight
 Away in yon infinite world :
The comet arrayed in leagues of light,
Unheeded by some from its lonely height,
 To the deepest abyss may be hurled !

And so may that sweet angelic face,
That leaves in my breast a vacant space—
 For it captures unconscious my heart—
Be seen by some who would not embrace
That lovely form that could fill a place
 'Mid the costliest productions of art.

I envy not the passionless soul
That could see this face and yet control
　　His heart for a solitary day :
To me 'tis ecstasy's utmost goal
To see that fiery eyeball roll,
　　And be thrilled by its joy-giving ray!

THE ORB OF NIGHT.

　　Slowly through the azure
　　　　Glides yon orb of night,
　　Silently dispensing
　　　　Soft and silvery light.

　　Gilding with her radiance
　　　　Every passing cloud,
　　Of her isolation
　　　　Well may she be proud.

THE ORB OF NIGHT.

Far above earth's tempests
   In unbounded space,
Wheels fair Luna onward
   With her smiling face.

On the sterile desert,
   And the snow-capped hills
She her silent splendours
   Copiously distills.

Fair and awe-inspiring,
   As indeed thou art,
Thou shalt ne'er have homage
   From this happy heart.

He who marks thy pathway
   Through the shades of night,
Will my soul guide safely
   Far above thy height.

When thy light is faded,
   When thy race is run,
I shall see the brightness
   Of the Living Sun!

THE LIGHT OF EDEN.

When the blazing lightning
   Through creation flies
And all matter, trembling,
   Into chaos dies—

I shall watch serenely
   From the hills on high
That great conflagration
   With unclouded eye!

FINIS.

www.ingramcontent.com/pod-product-compliance
Lightning Source LLC
Chambersburg PA
CBHW030400170426
43202CB00010B/1442